THE ART OF SHOOTING BASKETS

FROM THE FREE THROW TO THE SLAM DUNK

THE ART OF SHOOTING BASKETS

FROM THE FREE THROW TO THE SLAM DUNK

Ted St. Martin
with Frank Frangie

CB

CONTEMPORARY
BOOKS
CHICAGO

Library of Congress Cataloging-in-Publication Data

St. Martin, Ted.
    The art of shooting baskets : from the free throw to the slam
dunk / Ted St. Martin with Frank Frangie.
       p.   cm.
    Includes index.
    ISBN 0-8092-4009-2
    1. Basketball—Offense.   I. Frangie, Frank.   II. Title.
GV889.S68   1992
796.323′2—dc20   92-20264
                                           CIP

Published by Contemporary Books, Inc.
Two Prudential Plaza, Chicago, Illinois 60601-6790
Manufactured in the United States of America
International Standard Book Number: 0-8092-4009-2

To the most important people in my life,
beginning with the Lord Jesus and His Blessed Mother
as well as my wife, Barbara,
and all of our children and family

T.S.M.

To the good Lord
and to my lovely wife, Susanne

F.F.

CONTENTS

ACKNOWLEDGMENTS

Special thanks to the *Florida Times-Union* for allowing Frank to share his talents; to Glen Langston and former collegiate star Grayson Marshall, one of the all-time assist leaders in the Atlantic Coast Conference, for appearing in the photos; to editor Ken Gladstone, also of the *Times-Union*, for his work on the book, and to photographer Russell Phillips for providing the illustrations.

FOREWORD

One of the most neglected skills in the game of basketball is the art of free-throw shooting. Why do I say this? It is the only offensive skill in the sport where you're allowed to succeed without interference from a defender. Additionally, you always get to take the shot from the same distance.

Another reason why I am bothered by a lack of proficiency in this area is that you do not need to be a great basketball player to be a great free-throw shooter. I formed this opinion a long time ago . . .

I remember the day vividly. Back in my early days as a pro, I was a guest on Mike Douglas's television show in Philadelphia, and Mike asked me to demonstrate my two-handed underhand free-throw technique. He then asked if anyone in the studio audience would like to challenge me. Well, my first challenger was a short man who certainly didn't look like a great basketball player. This man then proceeded to make one free throw after another . . . after another . . . after another . . . after another. Mike started laughing at my reaction and finally let me in on the joke.

The man was Ted St. Martin, holder of the world record of 2,036 consecutive free throws. Anyway, the joke turned out to be a very pleasant experience, because over the years Ted and I have developed a friendship and a dedication to developing great free-throw shooters.

There are different ways to do a lot of things in life, and shooting is no exception. Regardless of your shooting style, there are basic fundamentals that hold true. If you want to perfect your shooting, and especially your free-throw shooting, you must learn these fundamentals. Only then will you gain the confidence necessary to be a great shooter.

This book provides an excellent means of learning Ted's successful style of shooting. I wish you well in your efforts to become proficient at my favorite basketball skill.

Rick Barry
Former NBA All-Star

FOREWORD

Anyone interested in basketball and dedicated to excellence should read this book by Ted St. Martin. His many unbelievable world records in free-throw consistency speak for themselves. I have known Ted for almost 20 years and certainly admire his many achievements—his hard work, concentration, and practice techniques should be an inspiration to anyone who wishes to improve or is just a true basketball fan.

Bill Sharman
Former NBA All-Star and coach

PREFACE

I know what you're thinking: How can a 5'7", 56-year-old man with no college or professional basketball playing or coaching experience possibly teach me to shoot?

I choose to answer that with a little self-history.

Growing up in the Yakima Valley of Washington state, in a small city called Selah, I remember taking my first shot at the basket at a neighbor's house. The goal in the yard probably was regulation size but at the time seemed much higher to me. The rim had a worn gunny sack or potato sack for the net.

I will never forget the thrill of the first shot that went in. I became addicted to shooting baskets. I didn't know why, but it was magical. I just knew I had to take every opportunity available to shoot. And shoot. And shoot.

I took advantage of every chance to go next door and shoot. My older brothers, Jerry and Larry, eventually put up a hoop in our yard. From that point we all played, taking more interest in the game of "Horse" than any other game. Jerry would shoot his right-handed hook shot from anywhere. I don't think he attempted any other shot. Larry shot his hook left-handed, but he also shot set shots. All the while I was developing range, shooting set shots from all over the court. Even though I was younger, the only way they could beat me was with those hook shots. Soon, as a matter of survival, I learned to shoot right-handed and left-handed hook shots.

The hook-shot experience only heightened my addiction. My love for shooting baskets was so great that I often pushed the snow away from the goal on winter mornings so I could shoot. I would shoot baskets until my fingers were numb with cold, go inside to warm them up, and then go back outside and shoot some more. I took shooting very seriously. The more I shot the more my shooting improved; the more it improved, the more I enjoyed it.

When I shot in our backyard I pretended every shot was the winning basket, just like any other kid. I wonder how many game winners I made on that goal at our house? Probably thousands. And isn't it funny—every time I missed, I had time for a rebound and a follow? The clock was good to me. But I really believe that is a terrific way to better yourself as a shooter: simulate critical situations.

The principal at Sunset School, Dyke Willoughby, was a great guy—terrific with kids. He even shot baskets with us

◀Here I'm shooting during halftime of a Florida State-Jacksonville game in Jacksonville. (Photo by Ryals Lee, Jr.)

every now and then before school started or during lunch. He shot this one-handed, right-handed shot. And he could drill it. He'd let it go, say, "Back of the rim," and it would go in—almost every time. The experience fed my desire. If Dyke Willoughby, this highly respected man in the community, enjoyed shooting that much, then there was nothing wrong with my addiction. I kept on shooting.

As an eighth grader at Selah High, I entered a free-throw shooting contest for kids under 15. The contest was statewide, sponsored by the *Seattle Post Intelligencer*. I placed third in central Washington and, in the process, fell in love with the free throw.

A year later, I made the junior varsity team and all the shooting finally paid off. No, I wasn't the best ball handler or defensive player or rebounder. But because I could shoot, our coach, Reuben Stegmeier, allowed me to launch shots from anywhere on the court while cautioning my teammates not to shoot unless they were wide open within 15 feet of the basket.

The late '40s and early '50s were the days of the under-handed free throw. Coach Stegmeier mandated every player to shoot free throws underhanded—except me. One night in practice I stroked 30 in a row with the one-handed shot, 30 in a row with a two-handed shot, and 30 in a row shooting underhanded. The coach was astounded. "St. Martin can shoot them any way he wants," he said.

During my sophomore year, my family moved to a farm near Naches, about 12 miles from Selah, and I transferred to Naches High School. Then times got tough. My brother Larry had been drafted into the Army, so I decided to drop out of school to help run the family dairy farm. I had to promise that I'd go back to school the next year.

When I returned, as a sophomore, I was ineligible for one semester, which kept me off the basketball team. But Coach Jake Bork allowed me to practice with the team; I shot from what is now three-point range while the rest of the team worked on rebounding. The problem was that I made too many shots to be much help.

I went on to become a starter for the varsity team as a junior and senior. But I was never much of a factor offensively. My height, 5′6″, was finally catching up with me. My ball handling was still a problem, and I had difficulty creating my own shots. Consequently, I didn't shoot much. I excelled more on defense and outhustling everybody else on the floor. My playing style was to go after every loose ball and to never give up. As a senior I was voted Inspirational Player of the Year, which meant a lot to me.

I was managing a dairy in Riverdale, California, in 1971 when I decided to play city-league basketball. I hadn't played competitively in almost 20 years, but I found that I hadn't lost my touch. After the season I nailed a backboard to the barn and started practicing free throws. With my son Tommy and a friend rebounding for me, I made 210 in a row, missed one, then made 514 more. I knew nothing about the *Guinness Book of World Records* at the time, but I soon learned that according to Guinness the record for consecutive free throws was 144.

Realizing that unofficially I had shattered that record, I immediately began a plan to officially establish a new record. Bill Nicholson, athletic director at Riverdale High, let me use the school gym and offered to be the official witness. I set up a 24-hour free-throw shoot, figuring that would allow me plenty of time to break the record. Family and friends were there, and so was the media.

I hadn't counted on the pressure of nearing the record. I spent too much time thinking about that and not enough about the mechanics of the shot. I made more than 90 percent for the entire 24 hours, which was another goal I had set. But my longest consecutive streak was 86.

After that I tried to break the record every Wednesday night in the Riverdale High School gym. One of the problems I was having was that as I got close to the record, I would start seeing the seams of the basketball even though I was concentrating on the back of the rim. (I lined up the seams the same way each time, the way most ballplayers do). Then one night a friend told me to forget about the seams and shoot the darned thing. That was probably the best piece of free-throw shooting advice I've ever had.

Almost immediately I not only made 144 in a row but went up to 200 before missing. The record was now officially mine.

That was March 15, 1972. Soon afterward, AMF Voit gave me my first break by sponsoring me while I toured the country doing free-throw shooting exhibitions. My next record came on May 5, 1974, in Chicago—245 in a row. In just five months the number grew to 927. On February 21, 1975, I broke into four figures by making 1,238 in a row in Nampa, Idaho. One week later, while in Phoenix, Arizona, for a clinic with the Phoenix Suns and also a halftime challenge with Jerry Colangelo, then general manager of the Suns and a great shooter in his own right, I made a record 1,704 in a row.

But later in 1975 AMF Voit pulled the plug on its sponsorship, so my wife, Barbara, and I packed up and

My wife, Barbara, travels with me to my shooting shows all over the country.

headed for Florida, her native state, and wound up in Jacksonville, where I renewed my career in dairy-farm management. On some weekends and vacations I did promotions at shopping centers, national sports shows, or NBA and college games. On June 22, 1977, I shot for 24 hours and again made just over 90 percent—a total of 14,466 shots—from the foul line. Three days later, on June 25, in Jacksonville, I made 2,036 in a row—a world record that still stands. And I'm proud to say that the basketball I used to set that record is on display at the Basketball Hall of Fame, in Springfield, Massachusetts.

By 1980 I was receiving so many requests that Barbara and I again left dairy farming and made basketball shows our primary business. In 1986, Coors-Light Sports gave me a big boost by signing me as a performer. I have been sponsored by the Coors organization since then.

My most recent world records are timed events of 5 and 10 minutes of free-throw shooting. On January 27, 1990, during halftime of a junior college game in Jacksonville, I made 175 out of 185 in 10 minutes using one basketball with one rebounder. I also made 90 out of 97 in 5 minutes using one basketball.

For the past 20 years my basketball shows have consisted of challenging shooters of all ages, including NBA and college players. In the first 10 or 12 years I challenged as many as three hundred shooters a day. But in the past eight years I've begun to cut back on the number of challengers that I take on in one day: after a hundred, I'm ready to rest up for the next day. After all, I *am* a grandfather—Barbara and I have raised 14 children and, to date, have 28 grandchildren—and I think I'm entitled to an easier schedule.

In my travels I've had the privilege of meeting many of the game's greatest players. Shooting with NBA great Bill Sharman was a lot of fun. Bill was such a good shooter and competitor and has been a good friend over the years. I had always admired Rick Barry's ability to shoot the underhanded free throw, and I had a great time shooting with him on "The Mike Douglas Show" when we tricked him into thinking I was just a randomly selected shooter from the audience. As I have studied and worked to improve not just the free throw but all the shots in basketball, Rick has been a vital resource. He is one of the greatest shooters the game ever has known. I have also shot with the likes of John Havlicek, Walt Frazier, Clem Haskins, John Salley, Sam Perkins, Jo Jo White, Dick Van Arsdale, and Keith Erickson, and many others. Jerry Colangelo made me an honorary member of the Phoenix Suns and presented me with a Suns uniform. That was quite a thrill.

I often have been accused of shooting in pressureless situations. People say it's not like game conditions. But when you are billed as the world's most accurate shooter, you are not expected to miss. You have no place to warm up or take practice shots, and it can be pretty lonely standing on the foul line at halftime of a game with a packed house and no teammates to keep you company. You are expected to walk out on the court and make every shot. Now *that's* pressure.

Three years ago, for example, I did a halftime show at an NBA game in Toledo, Ohio, between the Detroit Pistons and the Boston Celtics. I was introduced by veteran sports-caster Chris Schenkel, who was the public-address an-nouncer for the game; he then introduced me to the TV announcer for the Celtics—it was the legendary Bob Cousy. By this time, the Celtics and the Pistons were back on the floor—and everybody knows who are on their rosters. Larry Bird's Celtics and Isiah Thomas's Pistons. I hadn't taken a shot yet, but now it was time to shoot with all those greats standing next to me. I would call that a pressure situation. I shot 20 shots and made 20 shots. Sometimes pressure makes a good performer perform better.

These days I am more involved in the teaching aspect of shooting—I will continue to entertain, but not as often. As more and more teams find out that foul shooting is indeed teachable, they are beginning to turn to me for instruction. Over the past few years I have worked one-on-one with many players of all ages. After a lifetime of study-ing the basics of good shooting and watching literally hun-dreds of thousands of shooters, I have learned to spot a shooting flaw in an instant. I can recommend adjustments that will produce better shooters.

In March of 1991, Coach Rich Haddad of Jacksonville University asked me to help his team with their foul shooting. They were the poorest shooting team in the Sun Belt Conference, averaging about 50 percent. By the time my schedule allowed me to join their practices, they had only four games left in the season. I worked one-on-one with each player, looking for little flaws in his mechanics. Most players are receptive to a change that will help them be better shooters. The results were immediate: JU shot nearly 70 percent the last four games—still not good enough but much better than 50 percent.

Players need to realize that the learning process never ends, particularly regarding a skill like free-throw shooting. The greatest athletes in the world still take a lesson from time to time. What makes basketball players any different?

INTRODUCTION

You've been there a zillion times—perhaps in reality, perhaps only in your mind. Every basketball player alive knows the scenario. Each has lived it, acted it out on the playground, or dreamed about it.

You feel so alone despite the crowded, noisy arena. You gingerly toe the line, careful not to touch it and risk a violation on this crucial, nerve-wracking free throw.

Your knees aren't nearly as steady as you would like. Your eyes are having difficulty focusing. Still, you can make out the lights on the scoreboard, barely visible through the sea of enemy arms waving back and forth behind the basket. They tell the tense story you already know: your team trails by one with one second to play.

The noise is deafening. But you work to block it out, just like you promised yourself you would all those years while you waited for this chance. Finally, after the time-out called by the other team's coach to ice you, the official blows the whistle. It somehow sounds more like a train whistle shrieking loudly in your ears. At last he hands you the ball and extends both arms out to the sides with the index finger on each hand raised.

The signal tells the crowd what they already know, that this is a one-and-one free-throw situation: you must hit the first free throw to get the second. To you, the message is simple: miss the first one and you are the goat. Those enemy fans all want you to miss. They surely didn't come to see some player on the visiting team calmly swish two free throws in the final second and send them home in misery.

But you have blocked that out—or so you think. Now you are ready. You bounce the ball once, twice, three times, trying desperately to relax. You can only do so much. But your palms are still sweaty, your heart is racing, and your knees are unsteady. This is only a free throw, you tell yourself. I've made 79 trillion of these in practice. Bend the knees. Keep your elbow in. Stroke the darn thing!

You flex, rest the ball. The opponent next to you is chattering. "You're nothing," he says. "You got no game, man." It is his last desperate attempt to unnerve you. But you block it out. It's just you and the rim. You let it fly.

Then it happens. The ball is low and off-center, rotating poorly before barely nudging the rim on the left side and caroming weakly to the defensive rebounder. He tosses the ball high into the air as the buzzer sounds, the players on the other team hug, the crowd roars and rejoices.

You are sick. How could this happen? You know you are a 76 percent free-throw shooter, a statistic that the basketball society tells you is pretty darned good. But if it is, how could this happen? How could you miss so badly?

Your closest friend on the team comes over, puts his arm around you, and reminds you there will be another day. It seems like he's trying to convince himself as he consoles you. But you know. You know this was a wide-open 15 footer with no defender capable of stopping you.

And you blew it.

I've seen far too many players at the free-throw line with a chance to be a hero but who instead go home a goat. I know about the pain and the emptiness, the sleepless nights that follow.

I can help you avoid this depressing scenario. You can make that shot as easy as it was in practice the night before when you made 21 in a row.

For the past 35 years I have studied the art of shooting a basketball, concentrating on the free throw but working on all aspects of shooting. I'm 5′7″, not a great leaper, and not overly quick, so there was never a place in the game for me.

But there is a place for you, provided you are a great shooter. Not a better-than-average shooter—that works only if you are 6′7″, 230 pounds, and possess other skills. I'm talking about being a *great* shooter.

In the chapters to come, we are going to examine the finer points of shooting a basketball. I will take you step-by-step through all the shots and the variations: the slam dunk, the jump shot, the fast-break lay-up, the hook, the three-pointer, and, of course, the free throw. In my opinion the free throw is the most important shot in basketball: more games are won or lost from the foul line than anywhere else. It is a very teachable skill—professionals should always shoot 90 percent or better from the line.

The shooting theories outlined in this book have

worked for me and others for years. I've never believed there is a limit to how good a shooter can be. If you're willing to devote the right amount of time and effort, I'm confident that these theories will make you a far better shooter—the best shooter you can be.*

---

*I have used the words "he," "him," and "his" only for the sake of convenience—my shooting techniques apply to women as well as men.

1
BACK TO BASICS

Basketball originated as a game in which players tried to toss a ball into a peach basket. There were no other important components to the sport James Naismith invented and first introduced in Springfield, Massachusetts—no gimmick defenses, no high-post or low-post offenses, no half-court, quarter-court, or full-court presses. It was a simple game, really: just put the ball into the basket.

Today, basketball is played on a 94-foot-long court between two 10-foot-high steel rims with nylon netting bolted to a square, fiberglass backboard. Strategists dressed in $500 suits have turned the court into a chessboard, exhorting their players to execute everything from a pick-and-roll to a back-door cut to an alley-oop slam dunk.

But no matter how you interpret this dizzying evolution,

the success of today's teams still is based on the same basic premise: getting the basketball through the hoop. From the free throw and the jump shot to the lay-up and the slam dunk, there is no more important skill in the game than shooting. Michael Jordan did not win the NBA's Most Valuable Player award in 1991 because of his rebounding or defense or passing or ball handling, although he does all quite well. He won the MVP primarily because he led the World Champion Chicago Bulls—as well as the rest of the NBA—in scoring.

Regardless of the shot, players must be mentally as well as physically prepared. Free-throw shooting involves exceptional focusing and concentration and the ability to find that comfortable stroke and repeat it again and again. Shooting from the field requires, in addition to these skills, the discipline to make split-second decisions regarding what shot to take and when to take it.

The one-handed set shot is used today primarily as a free-throw technique or a means to launch a three-point attempt. But even though it is used infrequently while the clock is running, it is the basis for the jump shot, the most prevalent shot in basketball, as well as the free throw, the three-pointer, and even certain lay-ups.

Although all of the basic shots in basketball are closely related, I have devoted a separate chapter to each: the free throw, the jump shot, the lay-up, the hook, and the slam dunk. And I have analyzed the techniques of each shot using the following essentials:

Focus

Where are you looking when you shoot a basketball? Your eyes should be on the back of the rim at all times. When you are looking at the back of the rim, you are actually looking into the basket. Many coaches teach players to focus on the front of the rim; but if you do, you have to shoot over your target to be successful. You should always shoot at, not beyond, your target, the same as a marksman would.

Position

Are you aligned correctly, whether on the foul line or facing the basket on a jump shot? If you are a right-handed shooter, your right foot should be pointed directly at the middle of the basket and, in the case of a foul shot, in the middle of the free-throw line, slightly ahead of your left foot. Most important, you must be comfortable in your position. Remember, you want to develop consistency, which comes from routine, which comes from feeling comfortable and natural.

Grip

Hold the ball gingerly in the fingers and upper part of the hands, never in the palms. There should always be some air between the hand and the ball, allowing for a soft feel and ultimately, a soft touch on the shot. This is called fingertip control.

The Knees

I advocate very little bending of the knees on free throws. This applies mostly to free throws, but like every other facet of the shot, it must remain consistent each time you attempt it. The basic premise is that the simpler the shot, the least amount of unnecessary motion, the better the chance for consistency of routine.

Release and Follow-through

Your release should always be smooth and fluid, never jerky. A jerky motion causes a ball to be released quicker and therefore to travel faster. A ball traveling faster has less chance to work for you, that is, to gently fall through the rim if you do not hit dead center. The ball should roll off the upper part of the hand and then slide off the fingertips easily. If the ball leaves the hand from the palm, the shot cannot possibly hit the rim softly.

Arc

If your shot scoops in and out of the basket from front to back, that tells you your shot is too flat, that it lacks arc. This also prevents the shot from hanging softly on the rim if needed. At its highest point, a foul shot should be three-and-a-half to four feet above the rim. Shots taken from longer distances should be slightly higher.

Back to the Eyes

Are your eyes following the flight of the ball? This is a very common error. Never concentrate on the flight of the ball—shooters who watch the flight of the ball have a tendency to leave the target even before the ball is released, which obviously can't work.

Rotation

As with the arc, rotation varies depending on the distance from the basket when the shot is taken. A ball shot from the free-throw line, for example, should rotate in reverse one to one and a half times before it hits the basket. If you do not release the ball with proper backspin, the lack of rotation will cause the ball to carom off the rim instead of rolling into the basket.

Confidence

Proper practice breeds success, enough success breeds confidence, and confidence makes you believe in the process and want to practice more. It's a wonderful cycle. Most good shooters know they are going to make the shot. Always walk to the line, or spot up, or create your jumper with the confidence that you can make your shot.

Concentration

Are you missing shots because of distractions? Your shot should be so mechanical that it is routine business. You should know exactly what you are going to do, so the distractions that arise during the course of the game will never bother you.

I've never bought the theory of streaks and momentum in shooting. If you can make the shot once, then you can make it almost every time—if your preparation and mechanics are correct. That is why we are here. Read on.

2
FREE AND EASY

Games are often won and lost from the free-throw line. Yet I am amazed at the free-throw shooting percentages that basketball experts tolerate: at any level, 70 percent is generally considered acceptable, 75 percent good, 80 percent exceptional, and 85 percent or better the mark of a truly great player.

But that is bunk.

In my opinion, an NBA player who shoots less than 85 percent from the line is a disgrace. The average should be 85 to 87 percent. Good shooters should shoot 88 percent or better. Excellent shooters should be over 90 percent. I'm tired of hearing the announcers at NBA games say, "He's an excellent foul shooter. He's shooting 83 percent from the line."

That is not excellent by any means. That translates into missing 17 out of every 100 shots attempted. People tend to buy the excuse that players running up and down the court get fatigued during the course of a game and therefore can't be blamed for missing a foul shot. Give me a break! These guys are paid millions of dollars to play basketball and you're telling me they aren't in shape to run up and down the floor and then make a foul shot? That's kind of like an executive of a large corporation explaining that he made a poor business decision because he didn't get much sleep the night before. If a player is too tired to make a free throw, he is too tired to be in the game.

Players at the foul line are expected to succumb to mental pressure as well—a time-out called by the opposing coach right before the shot, taunting by other players, or screaming and waving madly by fans seated behind the basket. But it shouldn't matter. Players should use all of these distractions to their own advantage. If the fans are waving wildly, good shooters will realize that the rim and backboard are the only things in front of them that are not moving, which should help them focus in on the target. All that movement in the background seems to make the rim loom larger.

The time-out taken by the opposing coach just before the foul shot is designed to make players think too much about their shot and, therefore, make them more apt to miss. But good shooters use this time to avoid rushing, just as golfers wait for the wind to die down. Patience improves a skill.

Another common trick by opposing players is to shout or make some movement with their arms, legs, or body just as players are set to shoot. Again, good shooters use this as a reminder to concentrate, which could be even more difficult in quiet surroundings.

The ability to focus mentally—to use all these tricks, to turn disadvantages into advantages, and to relax in difficult situations—is based on one major attribute: confidence. Pure, unadulterated confidence. And the only way to unabashed confidence is knowing you will make that shot. That comes through knowing the techniques and how those techniques are practiced.

THE FREE THROW

Focus

It all begins with focusing on the proper target: the back of the rim. Most coaches teach shooters to aim for the *front* of the rim and to try to place the ball just over the front. But in order for a shooter to make the shot, he has to overshoot the target. Why focus on a target and then try to miss it? When you have a target, you should try to hit it straight on.

When you are looking at the back of the rim you are actually looking inside the basket, which is where you want the ball to go. Most missed shots fall short. This is because so many shooters shoot for the front of the rim. By contrast, shooters who concentrate on the back of the rim and have the proper arc on the ball rarely overshoot. When you look at the back of the rim, the goal even seems bigger because you are focusing on more of the basket. And who can't hit a big target more easily than a small one?

The free-throw shooter must focus on the very back portion of the rim.

Position

Your feet should be spread just far enough apart so that you can move in any direction with ease. For a right-hander, your right foot should be flush against the foul line, slightly ahead of the left foot, and pointed directly at the middle of the rim. It is critically important to do the same thing every time you go to the line.

Position your shooting foot directly on the foul line, a few inches ahead of the other foot. Both feet directly face the basket with the knees bent slightly.

Grip

Always grip the ball very gingerly as you begin your shot—like an egg, not like a lemon. The shot is as fragile as the outcome of a close game. Always remember that. You have seen many shots that don't swish but still go through the

Grip the ball gingerly, not tightly. Allow the ball to rest in the fingers, not the palms. You should be able to see space between the hand and the ball.

hoop. Your grip can have a lot to do with this: it can help slow the ball's approach to the basket so it will stay on the rim longer if it is off target. The longer it stays on the rim, the better the chance it will roll in.

For the one-handed shot, grip the ball with the tip of the index finger of the shooting hand exactly at the center of the plane of the ball. The thumb of the shooting hand should be spread to about a 60-degree angle to index finger. The helping hand should be on the side of the ball, with the fingers and thumb spread to full extension.

Assuming you are holding the ball with the seams running from left to right and the logo on the ball running in the same direction, this position is easy to establish. Once you have mastered your shot, every aspect will become mechanical, and you will automatically position your hands on the ball. Then you won't need to worry about where the seams and the logo are. (When you're holding the ball and not looking at it you really can't tell where the seams are, anyway—it feels the same regardless of how you hold the ball.)

In gripping the ball for a shot, always remember to hold the ball with only the fingers and the part of the hand immediately joining the fingers. Never hold the ball in the palms of your hands as you shoot. You should be able to see daylight between the basketball and the palm of your hand.

The Knees

Do not overbend. Many coaches insist on too much bending of the knees; on the contrary, only slight bending is necessary. Excessive body movements only increase the odds of missing your shot, especially in those clutch situations when

As you shoot, your heels leave the floor while your toes remain in contact with it. Never shoot flat-footed.

the opposing coach calls a time-out, hoping to affect your concentration and, ultimately, your routine. But if your routine involves no unnecessary body movements you can handle this type of situation much more easily. You should strive for a simple and fluid movement in your foul shot. Eliminate all unnecessary body and arm movements.

Release and Follow-through

The entire shot, from beginning through the follow-through, should be one continuous, fluid motion. You should practice this, even if at first your accuracy isn't very good. A soft touch plays a very important part in your routine: a smooth

Release the ball with a gentle, soft snap of the wrist when your arm and wrist are fully extended.

and fluid motion will help make the shots that hit the rim eventually fall through. You should raise your heels slightly—never shoot flat-footed.

Release the ball when the arm, wrist, and fingers of the shooting hand are fully extended. The wrist should snap slowly and smoothly, not in a jerky fashion—this gives the ball the necessary slight backspin. In the proper follow-through position, the wrist and the hand should be in the shape of a gooseneck.

Your follow-through should be complete. Even after the shot, keep your arm fully extended and your hand and wrist in a gooseneck position.

Notice that even as the ball is about to enter the basket, the shooter's arm is still fully extended.

Never drop your arms immediately after shooting, but instead keep them up in the air until the ball hits the rim and goes through. Anything short of this will result in jerky shots and missed baskets. I know keeping your hands held that high for that long seems strange. But trust me—it works.

Too much is made of keeping the shooting elbow tucked close to the body—"Elbow in! Elbow in!" is a favorite refrain of coaches. But it isn't that important. Remember—the shot is made with the *wrists*. The arms are used primarily to prepare the wrists to do the work. If you are already shooting well and are now comfortable with your elbow straight and aligned with the basket, that's fine. But if you're not accustomed to bringing your elbow in, don't do it if it is not comfortable. Comfort, provided it does not preclude other important basics, is of utmost importance.

Hold your arms at a comfortable height and in a comfortable posture. Your helping hand is on the side of the ball so that your thumbs almost touch. Do not be overly concerned with tucking in your shooting elbow. Use whatever position feels comfortable.

Arc

The ideal shot should have a good arc of three-and-a-half to four feet above the rim at its highest point. All the basics brought out in this book, along with a good release and follow-through, proper arc, and spin will give you that all-important soft touch. With it, if the shot does not swish, it will hit the rim and roll around and still drop through.

Back to the Eyes

Remember your focus point? Your eyes should remain focused on the back of the rim even as the ball is in flight. Do not let your eyes follow the flight of the ball. Whether you realize it or not, this affects your concentration. This is a very common error of which even many professional players are guilty.

Rotation

One to one-and-one-half turns of the ball, from the foul line to the basket, is sufficient. Too much spin will cause the ball to come out of the basket if the shot doesn't swish. Fingertip control is essential for good release because the fingertips are your last contact with the ball in the shooting process.

Confidence

If you ever go to the line unsure about whether you are going to make the free throw, you probably will miss it. Expect to make the shot. Be surprised when you don't.

Concentration

When you are taking a free throw, there will be five players on the floor hoping you don't make it and countless fans hoping the same thing, particularly if you are on the road. Don't be distracted. See your target and be so comfortable with your steps and routine that a bomb going off in the gym couldn't keep you from making that free throw.

HOW TO PRACTICE

Obviously, the best way to practice is by shooting free throws at a regulation hoop. Specialty baskets are available that return the ball to you, provided you make the shot, to assist your training. I have one and use it regularly. But there are other ways to work on shooting without the use of a basket.

If you are at home and don't have a basket, hold a ball with the proper grip and shoot it against the side of a wall. This will not help your targeting or arc, but it can assist other areas, such as comfort of position, grip, release, and follow-through. You can do the same while lying in bed at home by shooting the ball up in the air and catching it. Remember—each time you handle the ball, you should handle it properly.

I recommend that you shoot 500 free throws a day. This should only take about an hour (for me, 30 to 40 minutes)—a small price to pay if you *really* want to make yourself a better foul shooter.

Your confidence—which is critical—will gradually build as you practice all of these very necessary steps. I recommend that you take these fundamentals very seriously and practice each one, even if at first your accuracy isn't very good. You have to work at anything worthwhile in life, and foul shooting is no exception.

3
GETTING THE JUMP
ON THE OPPONENT

The jump shot is simply an evolution of the set shot that allows players to shoot over the outstretched arms of defenders. It is used now more than ever because defenders are bigger and more athletic than ever before. The jump shot developed as a counterpunch, a way for offensive players to offset the increasing abilities of defensive players.

Many of the basics for the jump shot are the same as for the set shot or free throw: the grip and the rotation of the ball, for example, are similar. But before we get into a step-by-step analysis of the jump shot, some differences should be considered.

The most obvious difference involves the amount of time to prepare. For the free throw you have as much time as you need; for the jump shot, relatively none. That means that all of the preparation must be done beforehand, through hours and hours of drills. The good shooter is fully prepared to launch the jumper—from either the dribble or a pass.

Proper trajectory, or arc, is every bit as important for the jump shot as for the free throw, but it is much more difficult to achieve. Almost every player who is struggling with his jump shot shoots the ball too flat. Even some better-than-average shooters shoot the ball too low. This is an easily correctable problem, but it involves the proper mental outlook.

The part of their game that players are most unwilling to change is their jump shot. Why? Probably because players develop their jumpers on the street, or in the gym, and become recognized by their style of shooting from the perimeter. You know a guy by his "J." ("Why should I change my 'J'? That's my calling card.")

It also may be your ticket out of basketball.

Be flexible! Be willing to change. In my opinion, the basketball establishment lets jump shooters off the hook in much the same way they do free-throw shooters. They say 55 percent is excellent. Stop it.

I firmly believe that players should make 60 percent of all jump shots from inside the three-point area and 50 percent from beyond it.

What about tough, off-balance shots? Simple. Don't take them. What about unusually long shots? You must know your range. If your maximum range is 15 feet, then don't attempt 18-footers. If you do, you'll wind up throwing the ball, not shooting it. And then it becomes impossible to maintain your mechanics.

Always strive to improve. You can't shoot too many jump shots a day on your own. Sure, I'm repeating what your coach already has told you, but some advice bears repeating. If a day at the beach is more important than spending two hours in the gym, fine. But always understand that it's an agreement you made with yourself. And when the scholarship offer or place in the draft doesn't come, don't be surprised.

Coaches bear some of the blame here, too. They seem to think basketball is a two-man game of chess. So much emphasis is put on other important skills—defensive footwork, boxing out for rebounds, ball handling—that the art of shooting the basketball is so often forgotten. Many coaches assume that players have spent most of their lives learning to shoot a jump shot on their own and that the coach's job is to teach the other things. This is true—to a degree. But if my team makes 50 baskets and yours makes 49 and everything else is equal, I win. Period.

I believe that too much emphasis is put on pounding the ball inside. Sure, good coaches make decisions based on their teams' strengths. So if the team is loaded with inside players, you pound it in. But that tends to put you at the mercy of the opposition's makeup. If it has a dominating defensive inside player, you may be forced into a less-familiar offensive attack. However, if you have five players adept at shooting 12- to 15-footers, it doesn't really matter how good the other team defends the interior. If all five players can shoot, you will score. And if the defense has to defend all five players on the perimeter, the chances are better that one can slip loose for an uncontested lay-up.

THE JUMP SHOT

Focus

Are your jump shots coming up short? You're not alone. Most missed jump shots in game situations are short of the target. Again, one of the reasons is because many shooters are taught to aim for the front of the rim, so being only slightly short will cause the shot to miss. Your target should be the back of the rim, allowing you to look into the basket, which is where this shot should land.

Position

Before you shoot, your shoulders should always be squared to the basket, but that will happen naturally if your feet are set properly. If you are dribbling, your feet (and consequently your shoulders) should face the basket well before you pick up your dribble and move the ball into a shooting position in your hands. If you are receiving a pass, face the passer head on, hands and fingers extended but relaxed. As you catch the pass, give with the ball and bring your hands closer to your body.

As you prepare to shoot, make sure that your feet are a comfortable distance apart, the shooting foot slightly ahead of the helping foot. The toes on both feet should be facing the rim, with the big toe of the lead foot pointed directly toward the center of the rim.

Grip

The grip is similar to that of the free throw: the index finger of the shooting hand is directly in the middle of the back of the ball, which is resting on the fingers; the helping hand is on the side of the ball, the thumb extended back toward the middle of the ball.

You should grip the ball a bit more tightly for a jump shot than you would for a free throw—jump shots, after all, aren't "free." But don't forget that the more gingerly you

For the jump shot position your feet so that your shooting foot is slightly ahead of your other foot. To do this, take your step, whether you are dribbling or receiving a pass, with your shooting foot.

The player attempting the shot off the dribble should begin to prepare his hands when he picks up his dribble and well before his feet are aligned.

For the spot-up shooter, the hands must be prepared
before the ball arrives. The good shooter has his
hands prepared to receive the pass while already beginning to position his feet in proper shooting align-
ment.

treat the basketball, the better will be your opportunity to
shoot it softly and, consequently, to make the shot.

The Knees

Remember that the knees do not need to be bent a great
deal—only a little more than when attempting a free throw.
Never bend the knees at more than a 45 degree angle. If you
do, you probably are more concerned with getting elevation
than you are with converting the shot, which should be the
bottom line.

The grip is similar to that of the free throw. Hold the ball a bit tighter, though, to prevent a defensive player from knocking it away.

Release and Follow-through

The arms should be held the same way they are for the free throw. Hold the ball just to the shooting side, close enough to the center of gravity to allow the wrists, not the arms, to do the work.

With the ball resting comfortably in the shooting position, transfer your weight from the balls of the feet to the

Before going up for your shot, square your shoulders so that your body faces the basket.

toes and begin your vertical leap. Do not lean backward or forward as you leap.

Good shooters know exactly how high their leap should be. Do not exaggerate your leap. If you go out of your way to jump higher early in the game, your jump shot will be released differently when your legs tire. The key is repetition—shooting each shot the same way.

Focusing on the back of the rim, begin your vertical leap by jumping off the balls of both feet. Jump straight up, not to the front or the back, and reach a comfortable height before releasing your shot.

The after-the-shot mechanics are the same here as in the free throw. Keep your hand at the point it was at when the shot was released, stay focused on the target, and have enough, but not too much, rotation.

When you reach the apex of your leap, release the ball with a gentle snap of the wrist, not the arms. The ball should be released off the fingers, but the wrist should move only fast enough to get the ball to the basket with the proper rotation. If the wrist has to move too quickly, the ball will rotate too much. Your helping hand should no longer be in contact with the ball but should remain extended. Your shooting hand should also remain fully extended to complete the follow-through. Remember—you should be in no rush to bring the shooting hand back down.

Arc

Jump shots in the 6-to-15-foot range are no higher than three-and-a-half to four feet above the rim at their highest point. Shots taken from farther than 15 feet may require a higher arc. Shots from closer than 6 feet are covered later in the section on inside play.

Back to the Eyes

Never, under any circumstances, follow the flight of the ball. Instead, remain focused on your target: the back of the rim.

Rotation

As with free throws, on jump shots from 15 feet the ball should rotate a maximum of one-and-a-half turns. Naturally, as the distance of the shot increases, so does the ball's rotation. If your range allows you to shoot from 24 feet—the equivalent of an NBA three-pointer—the ball may rotate two and a half times.

Proper rotation on a soft shot allows the ball to work for you when it gets to the rim. A shot that rotates too much will bounce out; one that rotates properly will stay on the rim longer and has a better chance to roll in.

Confidence

If you let a jump shot go and think the second it leaves your hand that it is not going in, then it probably isn't. Good shooters know how the proper shot feels. Early in a game, particularly at an unfamiliar gym, you may launch some shots you think are going in but do not. Don't lose your confidence; keep expecting your shots to go in. Before long you will get accustomed to your surroundings and regain your touch.

Repetition is the key. If you have practiced the shot enough and have enough understanding of your body, your abilities, and the mechanics involved, you will know what shots you can make and will attempt only those shots. Good shooters know the feel of a good shot—that's confidence.

Concentration

Distractions abound when you attempt a jump shot. Some defenders will always try to get a hand in your face. Others will slap your elbow just before you release your shot. But if you understand your routine and if you are properly focused on your target, your only distraction should be physical contact, which, with any luck, will earn you a trip to the line.

VARIATIONS

Too often, young players will see more experienced players effectively execute off-balance shots—leaning in to draw a foul, for example, or fading away to avoid a defender—and will try to imitate these styles. While these might be fun to practice, they are harmful to the fundamentals and mechanics of good shooting.

The best baseball pitchers in the world didn't learn to throw curveballs and sliders until they had mastered the proper mechanics of a straight fastball. The same theory applies here. Learn, practice, understand, and perfect the fundamental jump shot; *then* you can work on variations.

THE THREE-POINTER

The three-point shot was brought into basketball to open up play in the lanes and to bring perimeter play back into the game. The high school and college three-point distance is 19 feet, 9 inches, the international three-pointer is 20 feet, 6 inches (both of these distances are measured from the front of the rim), and the NBA three-point distance is 23 feet, 9 inches (measured from the center of the basket). Coaches have varying ideas on how much the three-pointer should be used, but most agree that it has become difficult to win, particulary at the collegiate level, without one or two quality three-point shooters.

Because the three-point shot has become such an im-

For the three-point shot, the fundamentals remain the same. Remember to find the line and know the court well enough to remain behind it. Bend your knees a bit more and increase the arc of the shot to compensate for the added distance.

portant part of the game, coaches should drill it more often than they previously did. How many times have you seen a team desperately firing up three-pointers late in the game but missing badly? A team that is well drilled in three-point attempts doesn't have that problem.

For a player without terrific athletic ability three-point shooting may be a ticket to a scholarship. Practice it. The fundamentals are the same. Don't increase your range by changing your mechanics but rather by conditioning your body to allow you to shoot the three-pointer comfortably. If you have to leap higher or snap harder when you release the shot, your opportunity for success decreases greatly.

STAY AWAY FROM THE GLASS

My theory on the backboard is a simple one: don't use it.

Coaches preach backboard, backboard, backboard. And many shots—lay-ups, power moves around the basket—are executed more proficiently with the help of the glass. But I believe trying to use the backboard on a jump shot causes two disturbing occurrences:

- An altered shot. Focusing on the back of the rim—not the backboard—is one of the fundamentals of shooting. Any such sudden change in mechanics is bound to adversely affect a shot.

- Indecision. In a crucial situation, a shooter who regularly uses the backboard invariably will reach a point of indecision on a shot from a peculiar angle. Do I bank it or shoot it straight in? That indecision could be the difference in making the shot and missing it—and that shot could be the difference in the game.

Good baseball players know exactly what to do in all game situations. The same is true for basketball players. Never put yourself in a situation in which you aren't sure how you will react.

REPETITION

The bottom line in shooting jump shots, free throws—any shot, for that matter—is repetition. Understand the mechanics and the fundamentals, practice them, and allow them to become second nature. Great shooters can't necessarily tell you how high they jump on jump shots or where they hold their helping hand or how high the ball soars at its highest point. But you can recognize them because they always do it the same way.

Make that your goal: do it the same way every time. And if you do it properly, you will make more shots than ever before.

HOW TO PRACTICE

If you have only a ball and no regulation goal, you can still practice your mechanics—grip, leap, release, follow-through—by shooting against a wall. You can also use a wall to practice receiving passes and setting up to shoot. As the ball comes toward you, prepare your hands as we have discussed in this chapter, with the arms, hands, and fingers extended but relaxed. As the ball gets nearer, begin to pull your hands toward your body, and give with the reception.

If you do have access to a regulation goal, attempt 300 jump shots per day, provided your legs are conditioned to do so. (If your legs tire, do not continue shooting because you will be forced to alter your mechanics in order to make the shot.) Always practice shots closer to the basket first. Your first 50 shots should be from 10 to 12 feet. Then back up to 15 feet for your next 100. If your range allows, drop back to 18 feet for 100 more. Your final 50 shots can be three-point attempts.

4

LET THEM LAY

Lay-up, according to some, is an outdated term—you hear more about breakaways, power moves, finesse moves, and various slam dunks. Still, players do most of their scoring around the basket with some sort of a lay-up, regardless of what you call it.

I've already stated that I believe most coaches probably spend too much time, particularly in end-game situations, trying to pound the ball inside instead of freeing up an open shooter. But in no way do I mean that players should be one dimensional—efficient from the perimeter but lost around the hoop. Every player—even the point guard—eventually faces the need to post up a defender. Players will be on the end of a breakaway. And every player will get loose inside for a freebie.

THE BREAKAWAY

Aside from the free throw, the breakaway lay-up—usually at the end of a fast break—is perhaps the easiest and least contested shot in basketball. But that appearance of simplicity makes the shot easy to take for granted. It is the only shot, for example, that demands ambidexterity. Players who cannot drive the basket with either hand are severely hampered. The steps and principles for inside play differ slightly from those for perimeter shooting.

Drive

As you approach the basket, be sure to use the foot opposite your shooting hand to propel yourself. Pushing off the ground with your left foot on a right-handed lay-up (or with your right foot on a left-handed lay-up) creates a better angle to the basket and also allows you to fully extend your right arm. Also, shooting the right-handed shot on the right side of the basket puts your body between the ball and any defender who manages to make up enough ground to be a factor in the play. (Defenders in a breakaway situation rarely will run to your ball-handling side but will almost always head toward the basket to defend from there.)

Leap

Your leap should begin with enough distance between yourself and the basket to allow a comfortable landing at or just beyond the basket. If you jump too soon, you will have to adjust your shot in midair, probably turning it into an off-balance jumper. If you jump too late, it will be difficult to get the shot off before the goal suddenly becomes another defender.

On the breakaway lay-up, begin your leap off of the nonshooting foot. Here, a right-handed shooter pushes off the ground with his left foot.

As you begin your ascent, hold the ball in front of you, with a hand on either side. As the ascent continues, use the helping hand to guide the ball into the shooting hand, which remains on the outside of the ball. By the time you take your helping hand away, centrifugal force will hold the ball in your shooting hand.

Release and Follow-through

The shot is the easy part. Turn your hand counterclockwise, making the back of the hand closest to the basket. Then use that hand to softly bank the ball off the backboard—aim for the top corner of the box on the shooting side—and into the basket.

Although I discourage the use of the backboard with the jumper, I prefer it with the lay-up. Because of your proximity to the basket and your forward momentum, you need the cushioning effect of the backboard to soften your shot before it hits the rim.

Momentum will take care of the follow-through on a breakaway lay-up, but the important thing to remember is to be smooth, not jerky.

THE REVERSE LAY-UP

Obviously, not every breakaway lay-up is so cut and dried. A defender occupying space near the side of the basket you are approaching, for example, may force you to reverse the ball. At times like this, the goal can set the best pick in basketball. Nobody is going to run through that pick.

The reverse lay-up is executed in pretty much the same way as the breakaway lay-up: you still push off on the foot opposite the shooting hand and bank the ball off the same spot on the glass. The key difference is that the step that precedes the leap should begin either directly on or even a fraction beyond the spot on the court just beneath the goal. The back of your shooting hand is now facing away from the goal, and the backboard is behind your head. With a gentle snap of the wrist, flip the ball back and bank it off the glass.

Gently bank the ball off the box on the backboard. Always use the backboard on a breakaway lay-up from the side.

In situations when you must lay the ball straight in, target the front of the rim and gently lay the ball just beyond it without using the backboard.

STRAIGHT DOWN THE MIDDLE

Breakaway situations sometimes require you to drive straight to the basket from the middle of the court. These situations, obviously, do not allow for the use of the backboard.

If you must go straight to the hoop, the mechanics are the same until the point of release. Then—and *only* then—the front of the rim becomes your target. Because of your momentum, using the back of the basket may cause you to overshoot. This is not the case in free throws or jump shots because fundamentals are correct; you will not be moving to or from the basket, but either standing on your toes or jumping straight up.

Because the momentum of the lay-up carries you *toward* the basket, unlike the jump or the free throw, the back of the goal should not be your target. Shooting for the back of the rim, particularly if you are moving rapidly, can cause the shot to go long.

THE POWER MOVE

The other type of lay-up is a power move by a post-up player—and that doesn't necessarily mean the big, burly center. Point guards, second guards, and small forwards do their share of posting up as well.

The drop step is a means by which a post player positions himself to score with a power move. It is designed to enable a player with his back to the basket to pivot in such a way that he outmaneuvers his defender and ends up facing the goal.

Begin with your back to the lane, feet just outside the blocks and a little more than shoulders' width apart. Both arms should be extended in front of you, with the fingers on each hand fully extended as well. This enables you to reach farther for an incoming, or entry, pass. The key pivot foot on the drop step is generally the foot closest to the baseline, although a drop step can be used to move into the lane as well. For the sake of explanation, we'll assume that you are on the right side of the basket, which would make the left foot the one closest to the baseline.

The beginning of the drop-step move: in this case the player is on the right side of the basket, so his left foot will be the pivot foot.

As you are receiving the pass, move your left foot directly back about six inches. As you catch the pass, shift all your weight onto the ball of that foot and pivot to your left 180 degrees until both feet are facing the basket. If you have executed the drop step and pivot properly, you now will be facing the basket, with the ball firmly held in both hands and your feet just barely in the lane. You will still be on the

Move your pivot foot behind your defender and shift your weight onto that foot.

balls of your feet, ready to begin your power move—either a lay-up or a two-handed dunk. The drop step is the best way to free a player to complete either of these shots.

A power lay-up involves many of the same mechanics used in a breakaway. Always remember to use the glass. A power move requires the player to go up strong; but going up strong requires greater momentum. The result is more need for the glass to soften the shot.

Pivot 180 degrees, square your feet and shoulders to the basket, and you are open for an easy lay-up or a slam dunk.

Drive

There isn't much of one. At this point you have freed your-self from your defender with an inside maneuver that places you in a position to launch the shot.

Leap

On power lay-ups, as on jump shots, your leap should be off both feet, not just one. Only here, it is important to jump as high as you can. On jump shots, remember, you should leap

On a power lay-up, jump off both feet and release your shot in much the same way you would a jump shot.

Close-up release for a power lay-up.

only to a comfortable height, one that you can reach every time. Here, the height of your jump is critical.

Protect the Ball

This is perhaps the most critical aspect of power moves. In this shot, unlike any other we've talked about and unlike any other in the game except the slam dunk, the ball is going through dangerous territory. More players will be close to you, meaning more hands will be trying to knock the ball away. Now is not the time for fingertip control.

As you begin your ascent, make sure you keep a firm grip on the ball with both hands. At the top of your jump, your body should be between your defenders and the ball. Always make the defenders go through your body to get to the ball; this often results in a foul and an opportunity for a three-point play.

Release and Follow-through

Your grip on the ball should be loosened by now, and the ball should ease its way to the fingers. Power moves, driving

As with the breakaway lay-up, you should bank the ball off the high, near corner of the box on the backboard.

Follow-through is similar to that of a jump shot. Allow your hands to stay in finished position until the ball begins to descend.

lay-ups, and other shots near the basket require ambidexterity, but with an added dimension. Here, you choose the hand based on the location of not only the basket but of your defender as well. A driving lay-up along the right baseline may best be completed by a quick, left-handed lay-up because the left hand will suddenly be the closest to the basket.

Confidence

Without going up strong, you can't effectively score on power moves, and without confidence, you can't go up strong. It is that simple. Aside from the mechanics, this is simply a matter of tenacity.

Concentration

At no other time during a game will you have more distractions than when you attempt to score near the basket. There will regularly be more than one defender working against you on power moves, and arms will be waving everywhere. You will get pushed, pulled, and banged, so focusing on what you are trying to accomplish is imperative.

HOW MANY SHOULD YOU EXPECT TO MAKE?

Throughout this book, I've talked about percentages. I'll be even tougher here. Your goal on lay-ups should be to shoot 100 percent. Is that possible? It should be. Remember, when you are fouled the attempt does not count. If you are not fouled, and you concentrate each instant throughout the shot and have thoroughly and methodically practiced the proper mechanics, the shot should be amazingly easy.

But practice and work in this area are as critical as they are in any phase of the game, including free throws.

HOW TO PRACTICE

The best way to practice lay-ups is by shooting lay-ups. Be sure to practice with both hands. If you have access to a court with baskets at both ends, work on breakaway lay-ups by going from basket to basket. Obviously, this is a terrific conditioning drill, but it also improves your basketball condition—that is, the condition while handling a ball. The best method is to begin with 20 lay-ups right-handed then do 20 left-handed, and finally 20 straight on.

5

GIVE HIM THE HOOK

A lot of players have the misconception that the hook shot is not for them. They mistakenly believe that the tallest player, the center who is parked underneath the basket, is the only player who can effectively use the hook shot. Even power forwards shy away from it.

Believe me, the hook shot is for all basketball players. Of all the shots in basketball, the hook shot is the hardest to defend. When I played high school basketball, even at 5′7″, I used the hook shot. How many times have you seen Magic Johnson make a hook shot at a crucial point of a game? Sure, it looks unorthodox in the era of power moves and power dunks. But if one of basketball's best guards—I know he is 6′9″, but he was still a guard—could use the shot, you can perfect it and use it as well.

Without a doubt, Kareem Abdul-Jabbar was the greatest and most well-known hook-shot artist. His famed sky hook was a thing of beauty, probably the last true finesse move by a big man—and it was virtually impossible to block.

The hook shot is a lost art, one that can improve a player's skills and usefulness to the team. But I do not encourage extensive use of the hook. In most situations the traditional jumper is your best option—it is the shot you practice the most. But there are some shooting situations when the hook may be your only choice. Let's say, for example, that you have the ball inside the paint with your back to the basket. The defender is directly behind you, and because of clogging in the lane there is no clear path to the hoop. You look but cannot find a cutter—a teammate breaking free. If your defender is overplaying, trying to deny entry into the post, then you are likely to have a free lane if he is not getting help-side defense. If he is, that means you are double-teamed and shouldn't be attempting the shot. But if the defender is behind you and is not getting help, the hook shot becomes a viable option—perhaps the best option.

The footwork varies, depending on which type of hook shot you are attempting: the traditional hook or the jump hook, also called the baby hook, that is used far more often in today's game.

THE TRADITIONAL HOOK

Position

With your back to the basket, take one step *parallel* to the basket with the foot opposite your shooting hand, and then pivot so that your shoulders are aligned with the basket. Push

On a traditional hook shot, push off with your non-shooting foot and bend your other leg to about a 45-degree angle.

off with the toes of your nonshooting foot and use your other foot for "climbing," much the same as you do on a lay-up. Leap only high enough to provide momentum for the shot—height of the jump is not all-important here.

Grip

As with the power move, because you will be in a very congested area inside the paint, it is imperative that you take good care of the ball. Grasp it firmly in both hands and keep it on the shooting side of your body, just above your hip. As you are coming up off your nonshooting foot, with the leg on your shooting side already in the air, your helping hand guides the ball into the shooting hand.

Begin the shot from near the hip on your shooting side.

Fully extend your shooting arm and swing it gently in a circular motion toward the basket with the ball resting in the palm of your hand.

Release and Follow-through

Gently swing your shooting arm, fully extended, in a circular motion toward the basket, the ball cradled in the palm. (Obviously, your body is not squared up to the basket.) When your arm is at its highest point above your head,

The mechanics of your follow-through—arm fully extended and hand and wrist in the gooseneck position—are the same as they are for the free throw and jump shot.

release the ball from your fingertips with a gentle snap of the wrist. Follow through by extending your hand and fingers in the familiar gooseneck position. Don't be in a rush to bring your arm back in. Allow it to stay in its completed position—and even exaggerate the position—to insure completeness of the motion and softness of the shot.

Your nonshooting foot, which you pushed off with, should begin to pivot toward the basket during your follow-through, so that at the end of the shot sequence your body is squared to the basket.

As with the jump shot and free throw, try to maintain a reasonable trajectory. For a six- to eight-foot shot, the arc should be no less than three feet above the basket at its highest point. I don't recommend the backboard for hook shots for the same reason I don't recommend using it for jump shots—it adds an unneeded variable.

Confidence

The hook is a specialty shot that not every player attempts. Before you attempt a hook shot, you must understand when to attempt it and, more important, when to forgo it and take a jump shot instead—or pass to an open teammate. The confident shooter knows these things.

Concentration

The hook is one of many shots frequently released in heavy traffic. The closer you are to the basket, the more attention you will attract. Stay focused and remember your mechanics, regardless of the distractions.

The hook shot involves so much body motion that it requires a great deal of practice. Because Kareem's hook seemed so effortless, we tend to take it for granted. But if you analyze the movements involved and realize that it has to be one continuous, fluid motion, you learn to appreciate the shot more and understand the time and effort it demands.

THE JUMP HOOK

The jump hook is today's answer to the conventional hook shot, a more jerky, compact variation of one of the game's oldest shots. Call this the abridged version.

The mechanics are fairly similar to those of the traditional hook: the ball is held firmly in both hands, the shoot-

The beginning of the jump hook is very similar to that of the traditional hook.

On the jump hook, however, you square your body to the basket as on a jump shot and leap off both feet.

ing arm is swung gently toward the basket, the shot is released from the fingers with a smooth snapping of the wrist, and the follow-through is still done with the arm fully extended and the hand in a gooseneck position.

Position

The major difference is the footwork.

Whereas the traditional hook is executed with the shoulders aligned with the basket, the jump hook begins in the same fashion as the jump shot, with the body squared to the basket and both feet facing the goal. You should jump off both feet, attempting more elevation than you would with a conventional hook. But remember—what matters most is that your leap is consistent.

Release and Follow-through

When you reach the top of the leap, your arm should be at its highest point above your head. Release the ball with a gentle snap of the wrist toward the basket. Then ease into your follow-through, allowing your arm to stay in position for an extra count, which aids the softness of the shot.

Confidence

The jump hook is a safe shot, difficult to block and, because it is taken from close to the goal, a relatively high percentage shot. So be confident. If you have practiced sufficiently, you will know you can make this shot.

Concentration

Any shot taken near the basket provides plenty of distractions. Stay focused on your goal, complete your follow-through, and be prepared to react to a miss.

Release the shot and follow through the same way you ▶ would on a traditional hook.

TIPS FOR SHOOTERS

In today's game you will see the jump hook much more often than the conventional hook, but neither shot should be forgotten. The most important point to remember is that all players—not just the big guys—can shoot the hook shot. And in the right situations, all players should.

Always know where your defenders are. Always attempt the traditional hook with your defender on your hip, which means on your nonshooting side. And on the jump hook make sure you are not falling away from the basket or falling toward it as you release your shot.

HOW TO PRACTICE

There are few drills to improve a hook shot other than shooting a hook shot. It's important to achieve proficiency from different spots around the lane and to do so with both hands. I recommend 50 to 100 hook shots per day for the shooter who plans to use the shot as a regular part of his arsenal. At least half those shots should be from the block— the bottom of the lane, which is where most hooks are attempted.

6
DUNK YOU
VERY MUCH

Slam dunking probably requires a better sense of the *how* and *when* of shooting than any other shot in the game. Miss a dunk when you could have easily scored with a lay-up and you can look forward to a friendly chat with your coach— actually, *he'll* be chatting and you'll be listening. On the other hand, there are times when your team needs a lift, when it has been listless and behind most of the game, and a lay-up would be a mere two points—but a vicious slam would bring the crowd and the team back to life.

Which brings us to slam-dunk rule number one: *Stay away from the dunk during a critical part of the game unless you can make the shot with ease.*

There are myriad styles and forms of dunks, from the

gliding, floating acrobatic efforts of Michael Jordan and Scottie Pippen to the menacing, powerful slams of Charles Barkley and Karl Malone. Dee Brown, a former Jacksonville University ballplayer whom I often saw play locally, won the 1991 NBA slam-dunk contest with a "no-look" dunk, actually covering his eyes with one arm and dunking with the other. For instructional purposes, however, slam dunks can be broken down into two categories: the power slam in a crowd and the breakaway at the end of a fast break. The mechanics are very similar to those for the lay-up.

THE BREAKAWAY SLAM DUNK

Position

Push off with the foot on the nonshooting side of the body. Distancing is all-important: if you come up short, the would-be dunk becomes a very awkward-looking lay-up attempt. If you go too far, the goal becomes a defender. And if you still try to dunk the ball after you have gone too far, you risk injury.

In a breakaway, your momentum and speed could cause you to mishandle the ball. So it's a good idea to hold the ball with both hands from the point you give up your dribble to the point when you begin the dunk.

As you begin your ascent, guide the ball into your shooting hand with your helping hand. Position the ball firmly in your palm, not your fingers. A ball held in the fingertips can fly out of the hand during a dunk attempt.

It is probably not a good idea to even attempt a dunk unless you can touch the rim with the area of your forearm two inches below your wrist.

On the breakaway slam dunk, push off toward the basket with your nonshooting foot just as you would on a breakaway lay-up.

Release and Follow-through

Propel the ball through the rim by snapping the wrist quickly, not gently, allowing the part of the hand where the palms meet the fingers to make contact with the rim as the ball slams through it. Try not to draw a technical foul by grabbing the rim—unless, of course, it is necessary to avoid injury. You'd rather give up the two points on technical free throws than blow out a knee.

Your contact with the rim may have altered your body's flight path, so be careful on your landing: it only takes one mishap to end a career.

Confidence

No shot in basketball requires more confidence and self-assurance than the slam dunk. There are no timid dunks. Remember—this shot is designed to do more than score two points—you could have done that with a lay-up. Here, you want to make a statement, perhaps change the momentum of

Protect the ball during your ascent. Use your helping hand to guide the ball into your dunking hand.

a game by getting a home crowd into the game or taking an opponents' crowd out of it. You can't do that without confidence.

Concentration

More hands will slap at you on a slam dunk than on any other shot. Go up strong but remain focused. Even after the release, you must remain focused to avoid injury on your landing. Don't look into the stands immediately after the dunk to see how well you have been received. Continue to take care of business.

At the highest point of your ascent, your arm should be fully extended with your palm directly behind the ball.

To complete the dunk, slam the ball through the hoop by snapping your wrist and allowing your fingers to come in contact with the rim as you release the ball.

THE POWER DUNK

Drive

You receive an entry pass in a post-up position with your back to the basket. Then you spin to face the goal, either with a drop step to get closer to the basket or a simple square-up move. From there, it is simply a matter of exploding toward the goal.

Protect the ball

This is more of a concern on a power dunk than on a breakaway. Because the shot develops out of your team's half-court offense, you can count on a lot of company inside the paint. Most of the defense will be in a position to slap at the ball as you begin your ascent—this will be its last chance to keep you from scoring.

The power dunk is much like the power lay-up. Go up strong, off both feet, in the same fashion. But instead of laying the ball in, complete the dunk by slamming it through the hoop with both hands.

Leap

Sometimes, the power dunk comes at the end of a lob pass, meaning that you must time your leap to reach its highest point when you catch the ball. But whether you receive the lob pass or get free by making your own move, you begin your leap the same way as you do on any power move to the basket: you push off both feet. And remember—don't attempt a dunk if there is a chance you cannot complete it.

Release and Follow-through

If you can please and excite the crowd, that's fine. But what's most important is the two points. Complete the dunk, then,

Again, allow your extended fingers to come in contact with the rim as you complete the shot.

in the same fashion you used to complete the breakaway dunk, but use two hands instead of one. Again, make sure the wrists are two inches above the rim. And slam the ball through with a quick snap of the wrists. There will still be a lot of bodies below you. If it is necessary to hang onto the rim for an extra half-second to regain your balance, do it. Don't showboat and become a gymnast. If you do, a technical could follow. But don't allow yourself to become injured, either. Ideally, you will ease to the ground, landing on both feet.

Confidence

The slam dunk is one of the most exciting features of the game. Fans love it; coaches appreciate it—*if* it's well timed. But as quickly as a well-timed, well-executed slam dunk can inspire a crowd and inject adrenaline into a listless team, a missed dunk can destroy momentum.

Concentration

You will be surrounded by defenders, hands will be slapping at the ball from all sides, and the noise level will most likely increase as the crowd anticipates your move. But you must stay focused on the task at hand. There is an obvious element of showmanship in the slam dunk, but that should always take a back seat to the business at hand.

HOW TO PRACTICE

Most great leapers, quite frankly, were born with that ability. But hard work in the weight room, particularly with squats and other lower-body exercises, certainly can improve your vertical leap.

Try to avoid hanging on the rim, which could result in a technical foul. But if that is the only way to avoid injury, do so to protect yourself. The technical is a small price to pay for avoiding an ankle or knee injury.

Apart from conditioning, the best way to practice dunks is to do so on a basket that is a comfortable height. If necessary, lower a basket to a reachable height so you can get the feel of the rim against your fingers and understand what type of dunks you are comfortable with. As your skills improve, raise the basket slightly, continuing to work on your skills. Ultimately, if you have the leaping ability, you will be able to take those skills to a regulation 10-foot goal.

7
MIND GAMES

Preparing yourself mentally for any task requires a clear head *and* a healthy body. For the game of basketball, mental preparedness is an absolute prerequisite. What does this mean? For starters, it means being drug-free. You cannot be under the influence of illegal drugs—and that includes steroids—and have a clear head *or* a healthy body. I won't turn this into an antidrug lecture, but this is a point that can't be overemphasized: *Stay away from any substances that alter your mind or your body!*

What does physical health have to do with mental preparation? A great deal. The body and the mind are meant to work together: the body must be able to execute the goals of the mind at all times. Your mind, for instance, may know that your body is capable of making a 12-footer from the baseline every time you come downcourt. However, if your body is poorly conditioned and your legs are gone, then the balance of your jump will be altered. Consequently, you will miss the shot. What happened? Your body lied to your mind—now your mind is confused. Get in condition and stay in condition and you will avoid this problem.

When I played, I really believed I could get every loose ball. I was a player of limited ability, so that type of effort was imperative. Everyone exerts the same amount of effort in shooting a basketball. But it is the effort in practice, the mental toughness that it takes to stay after practice an hour or two each day, that separates the great shooters from the average ones. Knowing you put the time in gives you a sense of confidence, and a confident shooter is a better shooter. Your skills soon become second nature.

Concentration is another critically important aspect of your mental preparation. Learn how to block out distractions: the spectators waving their arms, the loudmouth shouting obscenities, the player next to you trying to disturb you. You must be totally focused on your goal.

THERE IS NO "I" IN "TEAM"

Attitude is also critical. If you aren't in the proper frame of mind, you will only wind up frustrating yourself and your teammates. If you aren't willing to work hard, to sit down when told, to play when told, to take a charge, or give up the ball, the results will not be pleasant: you'll get benched, your playing time will dwindle, and your love for the game will slowly fade. Don't do that to yourself. You've worked too hard to get where you are.

Team play is more important for the shooter than perhaps any other player. Why? Because knowing *how* to shoot and knowing *when* to shoot are inseparable skills—the former is useless without the latter. This means understanding the game situation and your team's offensive priorities. If you are running out the clock, for example, don't attempt a bad shot. If you are trying to get an opposing player in foul trouble, pound it inside. If you deviate from your team's offensive tactics, you will most likely come out of the game. Then it won't matter how hard you've worked on your shooting mechanics. You can't stroke that trey from the pine.

LISTEN UP

Learn to listen. When you stop listening, you stop learning. Players who have been in the game for 20 years are still learning and adjusting. If that weren't the case, why would experience ever matter in sports? Listening is useless, though, without the willingness to adapt. If a coach who knows the game tells you that you have too much palm on the ball, hear him out. His advice may not work for you, but honestly and fairly trying it can never hurt. The players who get better are the ones willing to *try* to get better.

Being a successful shooter, like any other challenge in life, demands proper mental preparation: working hard; understanding your roles, limitations, and abilities; staying poised and relaxed; and always having the willingness to listen and change. But most important, perhaps, is keeping basketball in its proper perspective. The game means a lot to you, but you should always remember that it *is* still a game.

8
TWENTY QUESTIONS

Throughout the 20 years that I have been on the road shooting, teaching, and meeting people, I must say I've fielded more than my share of questions on a wide range of topics, primarily about my techniques, my accomplishments, and my experiences. I believe my records and my shooting speak for themselves. But it's only natural for people to want more insight into who I am and what I am all about. Here are the 20 questions I am most often asked:

1. Why do shooters miss?

Each missed shot has to be analyzed in light of the basics: Was the ball gripped properly? Were the feet in correct position? Was the focus on the back of the rim? Were the knees bent too much? Was there too much body motion? Was the arc and rotation good? Was the release fluid with proper follow-through? Did the eyes follow the flight of the ball?

Missed shots can be traced to botched mechanics. Have a partner watch your work and tell you what you have done wrong. Unless a defensive player made you miss, you probably violated one of the principles of shooting.

2. How do you keep your concentration for such an extended period of time?

My shot has become so mechanical that concentration is not difficult. That is why I preach making the shot as routine and simple as possible.

But there are other reasons. You must stay in shape—no matter how willing your mind is, your body may not be. Growing up on a farm gave me a great deal of discipline and responsibility at an early age—this mental conditioning helps me to this day.

3. How do you stay conditioned to shoot so much?

I don't go to the gym, but I do have a regular regimen of push-ups. I now do 150 push-ups every day, but back when I had to do 24-hour shoot-a-thons, I trained by doing 800 push-ups (four sets of 200) a day.

4. Have you shot with the pros?

Yes—more of them than I could possibly name. The ones I remember best include Bill Sharman, Rick Barry, John Salley, John Havlicek, Sam Perkins, Clem Haskins, Artis

Gilmore, Walt Frazier, Jerry Colangelo, Keith Erickson, Moses Malone, and Dick Van Arsdale, to name a few. These were wonderful opportunities to talk to the pros and learn that they concentrate on the same principles I do—not necessarily the same target, but the same principles: simple mechanics, as little body motion as possible, focusing on the same target every time, doing the entire routine the same every time.

5. Apart from specific mechanics, what must shooters do to improve?

Attitude and hustle are critical. Lazy players ultimately make bad shooters. Sure, they may have some natural ability and can knock it out cold in a game of "Horse." But the shooters who aren't willing to give 100 percent, who won't work at their game with hustle and determination, usually are not the best shooters.

6. Can shooting really be taught?

Absolutely. I have spent my life doing it. When it comes to shooting a basketball—the simple art of the shot—I believe I can teach with the best of them. I have spent my life learning all there is to learn about shooting.

I can educate a shooter about what makes shots go in, but how well he learns has to do with how much he studies. In this case, studying is practicing.

7. Why do some shots look so much different from others?

The technique I use to shoot free throws at shows appears very unconventional. It is a variation of the two-handed set shot, which was around when I was first learning the game in the late 1940s. The shot has an appearance of being released from the side, almost off the thumbs. But the shot I teach is the more conventional one-handed free throw.

My own style feels comfortable—I learned it at an early age, and I haven't changed it. However, the principles in-volved—targeting, grip, rotation, trajectory, follow-through—are the same for both styles. That is what counts. It doesn't matter how a shot looks as long as the basics are in place.

8. Who are the best shooters ever?

Calvin Murphy's 78 consecutive free throws remain an NBA record; Rick Barry's 90 percent is still the best career per-centage in league history. I've always thought that Bill Shar-man and Barry had the best form—almost no unnecessary body motion. Today, I think Larry Bird probably shoots the ball as well as anyone in the game. His follow-through and his focus are superb.

There is no better free-throw shooter in the game today than Ricky Pierce, of the Seattle Supersonics. His form, touch, release, and follow-through are perfect. If you want a role model who is playing right now, this guy is it. I predict that someday he will break Calvin Murphy's consecutive free-throw record.

9. Why don't NBA and college players shoot better percentages?

The easiest question yet. Players who struggle usually have a flaw or two, don't recognize it, and don't spend proper time trying to adjust. Shooting is like anything else. You have to work at it to perfect it. And you have to understand

what you are doing wrong. Quite frankly, most players just
don't do that.

10. Could you make all those shots if you had to shoot under pressure?

This question probably bothers me the most. No, the pressure I am under isn't exactly the same as game pressure. If a
player misses a critical free throw late in the game, nobody
on his team will be smiling. It is a tense time, often with big
money or big rewards on the line.

But remember—when you are billed as the world's
most accurate shooter, everyone expects you to make every
shot. I shot during halftime at all nine games of the Southeastern Conference tournament in 1987. I made every shot
for six consecutive games. By then, the crowd, about 17,000
strong, was rooting for me to miss. When I finally did, they
went wild. I was relieved but disappointed. Yes, that was
pressure.

11. How can you tell if a shot has enough arc?

If your shot misses by hitting the back of the rim and
bouncing straight back or scooping from front to back to
front, this indicates that you need to put more arc into your
shot.

12. How do you know if the rotation of the ball is correct?

Your fingertips should be the last part of your body to touch
the ball before you shoot it. At the point of release, as your
wrist is snapping, be sure the ball is going off your fingertips, not your fingers. If the ball comes off the middle of the
fingers instead of the tips, then it will rotate too much.

13. My coach constantly says, "Bend your knees more on free throws." How do you know how much to bend them?

To eliminate unnecessary body motion you should bend your knees as little as possible. Bend the knees slightly to allow the shot to be part of a fluid body motion, not a jerky one.

14. What are your thoughts on a designated foul shooter in the NBA?

I've been an advocate of this for many years. I think there would be less intentional fouling because the designated shooter would probably shoot at least 90 percent from the line. The big name players, particularly the good shooters, could stay in the game longer, just as the designated hitter does in baseball. Rick Barry would still be playing. I wish the rules committee would give this idea serious thought.

15. Why is the follow-through on the shot important?

Mainly, it helps give the shot a soft touch and, therefore, a better chance to go in. Without following through properly, an otherwise fluid shot will look jerky at the end. There is no point in being smooth for 80 percent of the shot and then ruining it at the end.

16. What if I'm 5'6" and the world tells me I'm too short to play basketball?

Mugsy Bogues is in the NBA and he is 5'3". And there are others. The bottom line is that if a player is efficient enough at his skills, there will be a place for him in the game of basketball. Take care of business in terms of practice and effort and you will find that lack of height really isn't a handicap at all.

17. Why shouldn't I use the backboard on a short jumper?

All of your other shots are aimed at the back of the rim, so why change things now? The rim is the same size and just as round from any angle. If you use the backboard some of the time and shoot for the rim some of the time, you invariably will have moments of indecision: Should I use the backboard or shoot straight for the rim? The last thing you need is indecision in your shooting, especially at a critical juncture in the game.

18. Television broadcasters are always saying, "He didn't set his feet, he wasn't squared up to the basket, that's why he missed." What does that mean and why is it important?

What that means, simply, is that you should not attempt a jump shot unless your body is directly facing the basket and your lead foot is pointing directly at the middle of the rim. If you try to shoot from any other position, your mechanics cannot be consistent. The broadcasters are right: shooters who aren't squared up to the basket generally do not shoot well.

19. Why are taller players usually poorer free-throw shooters?

I believe it is because they ultimately have more body movement, which, as I've explained, increases their margin for error. Coaches always say to bend the knees, but when seven-footers bend their knees, that's a lot of movement. Shooters who are that strong should need far less body movement, not more.

20. How soon will I start becoming a better shooter if I follow all your suggestions?

The first requirement is to understand that all of the techniques are important, not just one or two of them. Once you have firmly grasped the mechanics, the key is practicing them enough so that they become routine.

Anyone can ride a bicycle with no hands—but not on the first try. The more you ride it, the more comfortable you become and the more routine it becomes. Most riders can't explain how they can balance without their hands on the handlebars—they just feel their way through it.

You should practice these shooting mechanics until the entire motion feels natural, just like riding a bicycle with no hands. When that happens, you will find yourself improving remarkably quickly.

9

SKILLS AND DRILLS

I firmly believe there is a place for a shooting specialist in basketball. But no young player should believe that the only skills he must develop and improve are his shooting skills. If you cannot handle the ball, chances are you won't get many opportunities to shoot. If you lack effort and technique as a rebounder, your game is not as complete as it should be.

REBOUNDING

Regardless of how accurate shooters are, rebounding will always be an important part of the game. Face it—if you do not rebound well defensively and thus allow the other team to secure a rebound of its own missed shot, you are improving that team's scoring opportunities. A 33 percent shooter will score plenty if he gets three chances per trip downcourt.

Conversely, you can improve your team's chances of scoring by rebounding well offensively. How many times have your coaches told you to follow your shot? That's because it cannot be overemphasized. The more shots you allow yourself, the better will be your chance of scoring.

Defensive Rebounding

The beauty of defensive rebounding is that the game gives you a built-in advantage. Whether in a man-to-man or a zone defense, if you position yourself properly you will be closer to the basket than your opponent when you begin your pursuit of a rebound. Then, you simply block out your opponent. If you are in a man-to-man defense, identifying the player to block out is not a problem. If you are in a zone, be sure to identify the nearest potential offensive rebounder as quickly as possible.

To block, or box out, first turn your back to your opponent and face the basket. Your knees should be slightly bent and your arms out to your sides and also bent slightly, a stance which helps your balance but also helps you feel the player behind you if he attempts to go by you. Move your body slightly left or right if necessary to keep that player behind you. Also, give yourself proper spacing from the basket—I recommend three feet from the rim. If you are closer than that, the rebound probably will carom over your head.

With your opponent properly sealed off from the basket, you should time your leap so that you can grab the ball as soon as possible after it leaves the imaginary cylinder over the basket. Grab the rebound at the highest point of your jump, preferably with both hands, and hold it firmly. As you come down, keep the ball held high (no lower than your head) with your arms bent and your elbows out.

Never swing your elbows! Elbow swinging not only is a flagrant foul but also can result in serious injury. Keeping your elbows stationary still reduces the opportunity for an opposing player to take the ball from you.

Offensive Rebounding

The best way to secure offensive rebounds is to understand proper defensive rebounding techniques and how to combat them. Offensive rebound attempts, often from frustrated shooters who just missed, are one of the primary ways good players accumulate fouls too quickly and are ultimately disqualified.

The first rule is to remember to follow your shot. The best rule of thumb, unless you are at the shallowest point of your team's offensive attack and therefore must stay back to prevent an easy fast break, is to make sure your first step after you release your shot is toward the basket, not backward and away from it.

If you take that step and are boxed out, work hard to get around the player but without committing a foul. Unless the defender boxes you out perfectly, there will be an angle to the basket. Pick the angle that best suits you and try to achieve position, particularly if the ball caroms a second time off the rim.

If you are not the shooter but still are trying to get an offensive rebound, then you should work for position, at times even blocking out, with the same technique used by defensive players. The job is more difficult, however, because the defender has had a head start.

After securing an offensive rebound near the basket you become the dominant player. The most common mistake at this point is to attempt to dribble. Never put the ball on the floor if you rebound in traffic. You are already only a few feet from the basket, so why dribble? If you have a shot, take it. If you don't have a shot, pass the ball out immediately after the rebound. This greatly reduces the chances for defenders to steal the ball.

Rebounding Drills

The best way to practice rebounding is to throw the ball high off the backboard and rebound it at the highest point of your jump, remembering the correct positioning of your hands and elbows at the point of the rebound. If you are practicing with another player, set up on either side of the basket and bank to each other, practicing proper mechanics.

Teams often line up and do a variation of this drill as part of a pregame warm-up: each player grabs the rebound and, while still in the air, bounces the ball back off the backboard so the next player can do the same. The drill is continuous—the ball should never hit the ground.

BALL HANDLING

Precise ball handling not only helps you get in position to shoot but also helps you put other players in position to shoot as well. There is no magic to learning a good dribble—just like shooting, it takes a lot of practice and a lot of repetition. Here are a few tips: Never allow the dribble to raise above your waist—the higher the ball bounces, the better chances the defender has of knocking it away. Handle the ball firmly, even bouncing it harder at first than you normally would. And always dribble with your head up. Dribbling is kind of like driving a car in that respect: you must keep your eyes on the road so you'll know what lies ahead.

Passing

There is more to ball handling, though, than dribbling. Passing is an essential part of the game. Most field goals are a result of one or two passes—or more. Study the great championship teams and you will find teams that can pass.

The chest pass is the standard basketball pass. Hold the ball at chest height with your elbows in. Release the ball by snapping both wrists and rotating both hands to the outside in a motion that causes the fingers to fly forward and down. Always step toward the receiver when you pass.

And use your head. Make sure the receiver is open. If you are feeding the post from the wing, bounce the ball to the receiver. Entry passes to the post should almost always come from the wing, not the key.

Another type of pass is the baseball pass, used most often to send the ball at least half the length of the floor. The mechanics are much like those for throwing a baseball, hence the moniker. Face the target and throw a basic overhand pass, striding forward with the foot opposite your throwing hand as you release the ball.

The baseball pass, also known as the lob pass, is a good way to get the ball downcourt very quickly or to break a full-court press.

Ball-Handling Drills

Practice handling the ball with both hands, dribbling firmly, then do it while running, increasing your speed as your efficiency increases. As your skills improve, try spending several minutes at a time dribbling with your eyes closed, switching hands, turning your body, even running short distances. The ball should become an extension of your hand.

You should handle a basketball as often as possible—at night, during the day, whenever you can. The more familiar you are with your car, the better you will drive it. Handling a basketball is no different.

You don't need a basketball court to improve your ball-handling skills. In fact, players who practice handling the ball on hard dirt or grass actually can improve their skills by learning to handle uneven bounces.

10
PRACTICE, PRACTICE, PRACTICE

Throughout the book, I've talked about the specific mechanics as well as the mental and physical preparation needed to properly shoot a basketball. I am confident that these guidelines can help the poor shooter improve, can help the average shooter become a good shooter, and can help the good shooter become an outstanding shooter. But you can't expect to digest everything I've tried to teach by reading this book once, putting it down, and never addressing the concepts again.

You must practice to become better, regardless of what you are trying to improve. Those who take more practice time and work the hardest will improve the most. That is the simplest philosophy of all and perhaps the most important. What I want you to do is consistently work harder than the next guy—but also more intelligently. It is a formula that cannot fail.

Here is a step-by-step plan for organizing your practice time. I've followed this procedure for years to improve not only my free-throw shooting but overall shooting skills.

Identify the area of concern.

If you are struggling from the free-throw line, you must practice that portion of your game. If you need to improve from behind the three-point line, then that becomes your main area of concern.

Too often, players don't take the time to identify weak areas. Sometimes, the numbers tell the story for you. If you are shooting 58 percent from the line, for example, you know you need to improve. But what statistic is available to tell you that you are struggling with your power move inside the lane? Ask your coaches, your teammates. Find those areas where you need to improve.

Organize the time needed.

You know your schedule better than anyone else. Maybe the best time for you to work on your game is after practice; or maybe it's before practice. But be sure to identify that time and set it aside. And be prepared for schedule changes by choosing an alternative time.

Practice often.

I find that most shooters simply don't shoot enough. Some shooters who are struggling have decent mechanics but haven't worked enough, haven't done enough fine-tuning of the finer points to help themselves out of their slumps.

If a basket is not available, a wall becomes a practice aid. Get the feel of the ball and the shot by bouncing the ball off the wall, using your shooting technique.

I believe in establishing set practice regimens and adhering to them. If your problem area is free throws, I don't think 500 is an unreasonable number of free throws to shoot per day if you want to notice improvement quickly and make a new technique become routine. You can shoot 500 free throws in about an hour. But if you are too tired to shoot the shot correctly, you compensate by altering your mechanics. The important thing is to find a routine and stick to it.

My routine is simple: Free throws—500 per day. Inside moves, including dunks, short jumpers, and power lay-ups—

As you catch the ball off the wall, begin preparing your hands to shoot, just as you would when receiving a pass.

300 per day. Jump shot of 16 feet or more—150 per day. If you haven't planned and organized your time, your practice will become difficult. And if you haven't been committed to doing it, it will become a drudgery. Remember, this takes work.

Shoot with a partner.

This is important for a number of reasons. Obviously, it gives a built-in rebounder so you don't have to chase all of your shots. Also, it gives you someone who can critique your shot, who can notice things that you cannot possibly notice without the help of videotape.

But perhaps the best advantage to shooting with a partner is that you have someone to log your progress. When you shoot by yourself, you must keep mental notes of shots made, shots attempted, and other observations. This method of monitoring your progress can be unreliable as well as distracting.

Handle the ball.

Whenever you have any free time—while you are lying in bed, while you are sitting around visiting with friends, while

Even when lying in bed, you can practice catching the ball in a shooting position and taking your shot.

you are by yourself—handle a ball. Put it in your hands, in your fingers. Handle it with both hands. Lie in bed and shoot the ball up in the air.

People may tell you that you are crazy, that you are a fanatic. Don't be deterred. Fanaticism in pursuit of perfection is no vice.

Visualize what you are doing.

There are times when your mind is free to wander. These are the times to visualize what you are trying to do with your shot. Imagine the ball resting lightly in your fingertips, the position of your helping hand and your knees. Picture the back of the rim, the ball sailing toward it, and your follow-through. Visualize every detail of your shot.

Finally, remember to work, work, work. Understand all the mechanics of the shot and practice those mechanics together—work on the *whole* shot. Be organized. Identify weaknesses and make a plan to correct them. And be diligent. None of this matters if you aren't willing to work.

11

COACHING THE GAME

After years of attending clinics, performing shows, and living in the basketball community, I've met some of the game's top coaches. And I remain impressed. And I know it sounds corny, but in 19 years of shooting basketballs for a living, I've never met a coach I didn't like. Every coach I've met has welcomed me warmly. Some have invited me to assist in practice sessions, and I have met others in social situations or during shows and promotions I've been involved in.

I met Louisiana State basketball coach Dale Brown at athletic director Joe Dean's house during the 1987 Southeastern Conference tournament. I enjoy listening to Brown's stories and remain amazed at the breadth of his knowledge. To have to work as hard as a college basketball coach does—the immense amount of time it takes to recruit and to serve as an administrator and a teacher—and to still have time to be so well informed is quite an accomplishment. Apart from that, I just like Dale—he is a personable and very spiritual guy.

I met Villanova's Rollie Massimino, who recently left Villanova to take over as head coach at UNLV, at the Maui Classic in 1989 and spent time with him and LSU's Dale Brown at the Hall of Fame basketball game in Springfield, Massachusetts, a year later. Besides being a nice guy, Rollie is a great coach. Somehow his teams always seem to make the tournaments and have winning records. His players respect and love him, and because of this they always play their best for him. A coach wants his players to be relaxed and to have fun playing the game. If you are too tough on players, they will be tight and not play as well. Rollie's teams always play relaxed, and his colorful coaching style makes him fun to watch as he guides his team from the sidelines.

Clem Haskins has been a very successful coach, first at Western Kentucky and now at Minnesota. Clem and I have been very good friends since we did some clinics together when he was playing for the Phoenix Suns. At that time my consecutive record was 200, and Clem told me he had made 200 in a row during his college days.

There are so many others: Harry Simmons, who coached at the University of Southern Colorado in Pueblo, was an outstanding coach with more than 700 victories. He was a disciplinarian, demanding the most from his players. Tom Nissalke is the only coach to be named coach of the year in both the NBA and the old ABA. He invited me in to one of the team's practices one day when he was coaching Jacksonville, in the Continental Basketball Association.

During free-throw drills, he began to get disgusted and finally blew his whistle. "I'll bet that old man sitting over there in the stands can shoot foul shots better than you," he said to his team. Then he hollered over to me, "Sir, would you please come here for a minute?"

The players figured out soon enough that this was a setup, but you could tell in Tom's eyes that improving his team's free-throw shooting was a very serious matter to him.

Notre Dame coach John McLeod is tremendously knowledgeable. We've worked numerous clinics together, and I think I've learned more about the game from him during each one. Lon Kruger, the Florida coach, is a super guy. This past season he was voted SEC Coach of the Year, a well-deserved honor. Lon teaches the fundamentals of the game as well as anyone in the business.

There are coaches who don't agree with my ideas. Lefty Irvin, a former LaSalle coach, is a friend but vehemently differs with some of my theories. For example, he thinks a shooter should never focus on the back of the rim but always on the front.

Still, the key to believing in coaches is understanding the time they spent learning the game and the honest effort they put forth in teaching it. I have more respect for basketball coaches than I do for people in just about any other walk of life.

But I still believe most coaches do not properly teach fundamentals of good shooting. I understand that there are many facets of the game and only so much time for teaching. But more has to be done.

The key, overall, is for coaches to believe that good shooting can and should be taught. Professional or highly regarded college coaches hold clinics and talk about defen-

sive footwork, ball handling, proper boxing out for rebounds, and so on. The young college coaches in attendance
lock that knowledge away and teach their players the same
principles. The high school coaches attending the college
coaches' workouts do the same. The same thing goes for the
junior high coaches and the grade school coaches.

The next thing you know, the players have learned
about playing defense and handling the ball and getting
rebounds. Terrific. But do they know any more about shooting? Probably not. Yeah, a high school coach somewhere
along the line probably saw a player shoot a few bricks and
yelled, "Get your elbow in." But did he really take time to
break down the shooting mistakes the player was making?
Probably not. For that matter, did the coach understand
what mistakes the shooter was making? Maybe not. We have
to do away with this myth that the players learn to shoot on
the playground and learn to play defense in practice. They
must learn to shoot from teachers who can help them.

All baseball teams have pitching coaches. Can you
imagine a team at any level—college, minor league, or major
league—without a coach who specifically works with the
pitchers? Basketball needs the same kind of coach. Is pitching more important to baseball than shooting is to basketball? I think not. Let's hire shooting coaches and improve
the shooting at every level. And when this is not feasible,
let's develop seminars for coaches to learn not only the
proper mechanics but the proper way to teach the mechanics.

I have found that most coaches are reluctant to step in
and correct an average shooter. Sure, the coach tries to help
the guy who is shooting 46 percent from the free-throw line.
But what about the 61 percent shooter? No, that is not very

good, yet you rarely see a coach spend quality time with that shooter. Do coaches realize that the 60 percent shooter can be an 80 percent shooter with a few minor changes? Or are they afraid to step in because they might make matters worse?

Coaches should make good shooting an absolute priority with their teams. All the tactical wizardry in the world— the high-tech offenses and defenses, the well-thought-out presses and zones, the well-drilled rebounding mechanics— adds up to nothing if your players can't put the ball in the hole. The best coaches in the world are the ones who listen and learn, which is what they expect their players to do. Learn about good shooting. And make a point to teach it.

12
THE GAME I LOVE

I've spent almost 45 years learning, perfecting, and teaching the art of shooting a basketball—and helping o.... do the same. Watching the gracefulness of the game's b.... players is a joy. Being a specialist, I watch with a closer eye than most fans do, admiring and adoring aspects of it and fidgeting restlessly at other times when I see parts of the game I could improve. I love the game. But I still would like to see a few changes made.

There was a time not too long ago in football when placekickers only made the team if they could do something else. Lou Groza was a great NFL kicker but also a lineman. George Blanda kicked when he wasn't playing quarterback. And so on. But then general managers and coaches discovered placekicking specialists—players who usually had soccer backgrounds and usually were too small to help the team in any other way.

What has happened? The game has improved. Football is a better sport because of kicking specialists. The world of football now welcomes athletes who previously wouldn't have had a chance to play the game. Field-goal percentage accuracy is higher than ever—so high that in 1989 the NCAA took the kicking tee away from placement specialists and in 1991 narrowed the goal posts dramatically.

Well, if kicking specialists have added so much to football, why can't shooting specialists do the same for basketball? I know it sounds radical. But how radical was the idea 25 years ago of allowing a baseball player to bat regularly but not play in the field? Now—like it or not—it is an integral part of the game: team batting statistics are better in the American League, which uses the designated hitter, and big-name players fans pay money to see stay in the game longer

Genetics took away the 5′8″, 140-pounder's chance to ever play football. The use of kicking specialists gave it back. Let's give that chance back to the 5′8″, 140-pounder who wants to play basketball. How would it be done? One way would be to allow a team a certain number of "designated" free throws per game that could be taken by the shooting specialist. There are kinks to work out, but I'd like to see the idea tried.

Unfortunately, people who suggest changes often are accused of lacking proper appreciation of the game, of its traditions and roots. But in my case, nothing could be further from the truth: nobody appreciates the beauty and the grace of this game more than I do. No one can be prouder than I am of basketball's rapid rise from a humble club sport to a dazzling game that is admired throughout the world. But the heart of basketball's appeal is the basic act of putting the ball through the hoop. That's why shooting is so important.

Take it from a 5'7" guy who has made his living shooting a basketball: shooting is an art. It can be your masterpiece.

INDEX